M000121242

HAWAII

Text by Bill Harris

Captions by Carol Cooper

Editorial Manager
Bron Kowal

Editor
Gillian Waugh

Designer
Philip Clucas MSIAD

Featuring the photography of
Øystein Klakegg, Andrew Heaps, Chris Swan and Ric Pattison

Production Director
Gerald Hughes

Production Manager
Trevor Hall

Editorial Director
David Gibbon

Publishing Director
Ted Smart

CLB 1781
Copyright © 1987 Colour Library Books Ltd.,
   Guildford, Surrey, England.
Printed and bound in Barcelona, Spain by Cronion, S.A.

All rights reserved. No part of this publication may be
reproduced, stored in a retrieval system, or transmitted
in any form or by any means, electronic, mechanical,
photocopying, recording or otherwise, without written
permission of the publisher and copyright holder.

Published 1987 by Arch Cape Press,
Distributed by Crown Publishers, Inc.
ISBN 0 517 63113 X
h g f e d c b a
Dep. Leg. B-17288-87

HAWAII

Text by
BILL HARRIS

ARCH CAPE PRESS
New York

In the style of architecture that builders of shopping centers and suburban housing call "Early American," a decoration in the form of a pineapple often appears over doorways and in fence posts. The symbolism of the pineapple goes back to the old whalers who took long voyages out of New England. When they returned home, they usually had a lot more on board than the products of whales they had found. They had exotic treasure from the South Seas and they had stories to tell as well. Naturally, their neighbors were interested, and so, as a sign that the captain was home and receiving visitors, a fresh pineapple was placed outside his front door. Eventually, as often happens, people began carving pineapples from wood or from stone as a more permanent sign of hospitality.

The pineapple is also one of the symbols of Hawaii; and that's entirely appropriate because so is hospitality.

James Michener has said that Hawaii's real flowers are its people. He said there are more conspicuously beautiful young women in Hawaii than anywhere else in the United States, and added that the young men are just as handsome. Anyone who's ever been there will agree with that, and probably vouch for the fact that they are among the warmest, most hospitable people on earth.

It hasn't always been exactly like that. When Captain James Cook, the first European to discover Hawaii, landed there in 1778, he was "pleasantly surprised" by the welcoming party that rowed out into the harbor to meet his ship. But the pleasure faded when the first shore party found that the natives were dedicated thieves. They weren't too subtle about it, either. They took oars, muskets, anything at all that wasn't tied down. And they wouldn't stop until one of them was shot by a sailor. With that shot, civilization officially arrived in the place Cook named the "Sandwich Islands."

The Polynesians Cook found there were of the same race he had found in far-off Tahiti. "How shall we account for this nation spreading itself over this vast ocean?" he wrote. And until this day, no one has been able to account for it. They thought Cook was their long-lost white god Lono, and when he went ashore for the first time, something happened that he had never seen before, even though he had been to, even discovered, some of the most exotic places in all the world. "The very instant I leaped ashore, they all fell flat on their faces," he recorded. A year later these same people killed Cook when he turned his back on them.

None of that is to say that Cook and others who followed him found all the native Hawaiians to be thieving, hostile savages. But they were a primitive people, and life for them was less than easy. Human sacrifices were common, the chiefs of the different islands kept them in an almost constant state of bloody war, and their chiefs were generally cruel men. In spite of it all, the Islanders were handsome and beautiful, childlike and trusting.

Mark Twain, who toured the Islands on horseback in the mid-19th century, explains what they were like and how they changed: "Human sacrifices were offered up in those old bygone days when the simple child of nature, yielding momentarily to sin when sorely tempted, acknowledged his error when calm reflection had shown it to him, and came forward with noble frankness and offered up his grandmother as an atoning sacrifice – in those old days when the luckless sinner could keep on cleansing his conscience and achieving periodical happiness as long as his relations held out; long before the missionaries braved a thousand privations to come and make them permanently miserable by telling them how beautiful and how blissful a place heaven is, and how nearly impossible it is to get there; and showed the poor native how dreary a place perdition is and what unnecessarily liberal facilities there are for going to it; showed him how, in his ignorance, he had gone and fooled away all his kinfolks to no purpose; showed him what rapture it is to work all day long for fifty cents to buy food for the next day with, as compared to fishing for a pastime and lolling in the shade through eternal summer, and eating the bounty that nobody labored to provide but Nature. How sad it is to think of the multitudes who went to their graves in this beautiful island and never knew there was a hell!"

"Paradise" is a word that's used more often than any other to describe the Hawaiian Islands. That's because no other word fits quite so well. It's not uncommon to hear tourists remark that if heaven isn't like this, they don't want to go there. And tourists are going to Hawaii in waves as spectacular as the seaborne waves that break on those fabulous beaches. About three million visitors arrive in Hawaii every year, mostly from the United States. But of the million-plus Japanese tourists who visit the United States every year, 75 percent go to Hawaii. Japanese-Americans rank second in numbers behind "Haole," the name native Hawaiians use for mainland whites, so visitors from Japan feel right at home. Just as important, probably, is the fact that Honolulu is just six jet hours from Tokyo.

The jet plane is what's behind the Hawaiian tourist boom. Back in the 1950s, when Hawaii became a state, most Americans ·who went there were from California, and most of them went by boat. It was a leisurely, unforgettable experience for them. One man, who made the trip several times, describes it this way:

"On the fourth morning out from San Francisco, you'd wake up to see Molokai there on the left and Oahu on the right. Rounding Diamond Head, the biggest thing on the island looked to be a pink Moorish palace, the Royal Hawaiian Hotel.

"The ship would take on three tugloads of greeters, and move on to the dock at Aloha Tower, where the Royal Hawaiian Band and hula girls met you."

The weekly arrival of the big white ship "Lurline" from San Francisco was called "Steamer Day" in the Honolulu of the '50s. The mainlanders, who had invested five days to get there, got a welcome that was unrivalled anywhere in the world. The air was perfumed with the heavy scent of tropical flowers, the green mountains accented the dramatic cliffs, and the beautiful white beaches presented a picture that could only conjure up that same word again, "paradise."

And to add pleasure to the paradise, the mainlanders were met by those beautiful hula girls singing the love songs of their Polynesian ancestors, while in the water below the slowly moving ship, native divers raced to the bottom of the crystal clear harbor to retrieve silver dollars tossed overboard by the visitors. It put everyone in the mood for a party, and it wasn't uncommon for the party to last until the following day, when the famous Hawaiian sun lured everyone down to the beach.

People who go to Hawaii today get there faster and spend less time getting acclimated when they do. But the legendary hospitality that is Hawaii and the spectacular beauty make their first impression of the place just as memorable today as it ever was.

The Islands, flung like a strand of pearls into the middle of the Pacific Ocean, are about 2,500 miles from San Francisco. There are about 132 islands in all, some not inhabited at all, some the private preserves of single families. In total area, Hawaii is two-thirds the size of Sicily, but bigger than Massachusetts. The eight major islands in the southeast: Hawaii, Oahu, Maui, Kahoolawe, Kayai, Molokai and Niihau, make up all but three square miles of the total area. And of the major islands, one isn't inhabited at all. Kahoolawe is used by the military as a target island for bombing and artillery practice.

Honolulu and Pearl Harbor are on the island of Oahu, which is where some 80 percent of the state's population lives. The biggest island, Hawaii, is also the farthest south and, in fact, is the southernmost point in the United States, at the tip of Volcanoes National Park.

It's always spring in Hawaii because of the cooling winds from the Pacific, which keep the year round temperature in the neighborhood of 75°F. And the sun is shining just about all the time. The Islanders thank one of their gods, Maui, for that. They say that many years ago he hid in the forest until the sun came out. When it did, he lassoed it and tied it down so it couldn't move. The sun didn't like that very much, according to the legend, but Maui wouldn't let it go until it promised to move more slowly across his islands. A promise given is a promise kept when you're the sun. And the promise is still being kept all these centuries later.

If you were playing a word association game and someone said "Hawaii," it wouldn't be long before someone else said "Hula." Hawaii didn't have a written language before the missionaries came in the 19th century, and the tradition of the people was handed down through the movement of the hands in this graceful dance, much in the same way Africans kept the past alive with an oral tradition. In the very early days, the dance was done only by men. Women got into the act generations ago, of course, and that's another nice thing about Hawaii.

Hula schools in Hawaii are as popular as ballet schools in the rest of the country, and today boys as well as girls are learning it. It takes all forms, from a slow and sensual dance to the bump and grind associated with carnivals and waterfront bars. An agent in Honolulu, who provides dancers for weddings and bar mitzvahs, says, "the hula can be sexy as hell, but it should also be innocent as hell."

"All the dancers I've ever worked with," she says, "are extremely modest girls who would squeal like hell if a man walked into their dressing room while they were in bra and panties. But they think nothing of performing before an audience and shaking their hips in a Tahiti skirt cut several inches below the navel."

Another agent, who was asked to provide a topless hula dancer, found that none of the regular island dancers would do it. He solved the problem by going to the mainland for a dark-skinned girl who would.

What makes the hula something special is the complete innocence the dancers project, all the while moving their bodies in a decidedly sexual way. It isn't easy of course, and those girls from the mainland, dark-skinned or not, just can't duplicate it.

The legend of how the hula began, undoubtedly handed down in the language of dance, is that the sister of the fire goddess, Pele, was such a wonderful dancer that she mesmerized her sister into following her to the caves in the northern part of Oahu. Because of the wonder of it all, Pele is presumably still there.

Hula was a national institution when the missionaries arrived. An institution they didn't much care for! The shocked Christians from New England immediately set out to dress the hula girls in high-collared, long-sleeved blouses and long skirts. That took most of the fun out of it, and the dance died out rather quickly! In 1883, King Kalakaua brought it back as part of the ceremonies at his coronation. They danced 252 different kinds of hula for him! Which goes to show that you can't keep a good idea down forever!

Leis are as Hawaiian as the hula, and they're usually used as a sign of welcome or farewell. In the early days they were reserved for royalty, and they were always made from feathers. Today most are made of flowers, although in some quarters plastic seems to be considered fashionable. Sometimes they're made of white and yellow ginger blossoms that smell as beautiful as they look. Frangipani is another common lei flower. Its overlapping petals add a special beauty to the garland, and the aroma lets you know you're in the tropics. Carnations and orchids also make beautiful leis and add to the wide variety you can buy all over the islands from street vendors and flower shops.

If the hula and the lei are typically Hawaiian, so is the Polynesian language. But the language isn't exclusively Hawaiian. Indeed, when Captain Cook first landed there, he had no trouble talking with the natives, which pleased him no end because it made it possible for him to place a large order for provisions for his ship. Which, no doubt, pleased the natives no end! Cook had learned the language on Tahiti, where, incidentally, one of his ship's crew was killed and eaten for dinner by the natives.

Hawaii is the only state with its own language, and some of its words like "lanai," which means "porch," and "muumuu," a loose-fitting, non-revealing dress mandated by the missionaries, have become part of the basic language of the mainland. Every word in the Hawaiian language ends in a vowel. Consonants are never used without a vowel between them, but whole strings of vowels can come together. There's a basic rule that *a, e, i, o* and *u* are pronounced separately, but sometimes combinations like *au*, which gets pronounced like the *ow* in "cow," offer enough exceptions to keep you on your toes. The fact is, vowels are the mainstay of the Hawaiian language because they have only seven consonants to choose from. The ones they recognize are *h, k, l, m, n, p,* and *w.*

It all adds up to a very melodious-sounding language. Even the word for "anger," "huhu," makes you happy when you hear it. If a Hawaiian wants you to get a move on, the word for it is "wikiwiki." If that doesn't work, you'll probably be in "pilikia," "trouble."

The word "Kamaaina" is usually used to describe a native-born Hawaiian descended from the native chiefs or the missionaries. They have traditionally run the businesses of Hawaii, and figure prominently in the social structure of the islands. In the early days, native chiefs kept their position (and their heads) at the whim of the king. And the person of the king changed as frequently as the whim, so the land changed hands on a fairly regular basis. Descendants of the missionaries overthrew the traditional Hawaiian monarchy and introduced Western ideas about who owned what. King Kamehameha II went along with the new idea and convinced some 240 chiefs that they should, too. Their descendants are the "Kamaaina" of today.

But who were those missionaries who took

the word of paradise to paradise itself? There were ten groups of them, Calvinists all, who were sent out from Boston by the American Board of Commissioners for Foreign Missions to give the gift of Christianity to the heathen. They arrived in the early 19th century, 184-strong. Many of them died, more went home to New England. But 52 families, the strongest of the lot, stayed on to produce more than 5,000 descendants. And to change the course of Hawaiian history.

They didn't like what they found there. "Public nakedness and lewd dancing" were first on the agenda of things to be done away with, and they saw their job clearly: it wouldn't be enough to save sinners, they would have to civilize these savages at the same time.

It wasn't easy for the missionaries at first, but, as Yankee Calvinists, "easy" didn't matter much to them. Slowly they befriended the chiefs and members of the royal family, but they were never able to touch the soul of King Lihiliho. Then, one day, Liholiho decided to travel to London for a chat with his "friend," King George IV.

He wasn't gone long before the people of Hawaii were told not to do a thing, including lighting a fire, on the Sabbath. Before much longer, the chiefs and head men were ordered to make sure their people obeyed the new rule and, furthermore, attended both the church and the mission school. One chief refused and, unfortunately for him, his father died leaving all his land to the king. In retaliation for this affront, he decided to go to war with the government. And lost the battle.

The volunteers who defeated him had prayed to the Christian God, had refused to do battle on the Sabbath, and refrained from killing the rebel when it was all over. All this, plus the fact that they had done it without the leadership of the king, made them begin to take the ways of this new god a little more seriously.

Meanwhile, the king and the queen both died in London of measles, a common disease in Britain, but quite alien to this pair of "damned cannibals," as King George was heard to call them. They were returned home and buried with great ceremony by the Christians, even though the king had never accepted their church himself. This further impressed the chiefs, who were now eager to accept the teachings of the missionaries, and their people eagerly followed them.

The missionaries weren't the only white people on the islands in the 1800s. There were hunters and sailors and others who had little truck with these upright folk from Boston. The missionaries paid little attention to them, either, at first. But they began to notice the missionaries when the newly-Christianized chiefs began suppressing such things as drunkenness and debauchery, and, most important, the renting of women. At one point, a boatload of sailors actually attacked the home of one of the missionaries, who escaped with his life only because the Christian chiefs came to his rescue.

The U.S. Navy even intervened, telling the chiefs it wasn't unusual for civilized countries to allow prostitution. But Christian truth and Yankee perseverance won the day.

By the 1830s, the missionaries found that most of their troubles were behind them, and they were joined by a new breed of evangelists from New England whose brand of preaching "broke sinners down," and brought them to repentance with "the battle-axe of the Lord." In a single day in 1838, no less than 1,705 converts were baptized into what may have been the biggest Protestant congregation anywhere in the world.

It was only a matter of time before they became powerful in politics, too, and they used their influence to get American support for a Hawaii free from the influence of other foreign countries, especially Britain and France.

Then they began to buy the place.

In 1835, three young men from New England arrived in Honolulu. One of them had been a student at Yale Theological Seminary, but they didn't come to save souls. Their game, as it turned out, was real estate.

Within a few years, they made a secret agreement with the king that gave them exclusive rights to all unoccupied and undeveloped land in the islands. Then they set out to peddle those rights in the United States and Europe. Apparently their timing was wrong, because they couldn't find any interested buyers anywhere except in Belgium, and even that prospect finally died. Eventually their agent returned to Hawaii with a ticket he had no money to pay for.

The bankruptcy trials that followed were nasty and drove a wedge between the Western businessmen and the missionaries.

But through it all, the missionaries became convinced that land reform was essential and their role in it indispensable.

Under Hawaiian tradition, the common people had no rights in the land. The chiefs knew that land was power because it was the source of life. As one missionary wrote: "from Uka, mountain, whence came wood, kapa, for clothing, olona, for fish line, ti-leaf for wrapping paper, ie for rattan lashing, wild birds for food, to the sea, kai, whence came ia, fish, and all connected therewith," all the necessities of life were easily available to everyone.

The missionaries felt that industry and thrift were important virtues, and the only way to encourage those virtues in the common people was to allow them to become landowners. There were winds of change all over the world at that time and the chiefs knew they had to face the fact that they would come to them as well. They were slow to accept the idea though, and it wasn't until 1847 that commoners were allowed to buy their own land. The land division was called the Great Mahele. It allowed the king to retain vast estates for himself and for the chiefs to buy title to the land they already held. The big breakthrough was for the commoners, who were now allowed to buy tiny lots, called *kuleanas,* for themselves.

Foreigners weren't allowed to share in the Great Mahele, but could lease land for a period of 50 years. The Hawaiian people, meanwhile, bought their kuleanas by billing the government for services they had performed free for the king. The king's tailor, for instance, was given a lot in Nuuanu Valley. The man who piloted the king's ship got a town lot in Honolulu and about four acres in Waikiki!

It wasn't long, of course, before the law was changed to allow foreigners into the act. And that was the beginning of the end as far as the natives were concerned. The idea of the independent family farm never caught on with the Hawaiians. Taro was the main crop, and growing it was hard work. Now that they were free of their chiefs, they used the freedom to move away from them. They knew that the freedom to buy land also gave them the freedom to sell it, and that was the option they chose.

And guess who bought it from them? By the end of the 19th century, the white men owned four acres to every one acre of land owned by the native Hawaiians and their chiefs.

Property values in Hawaii today are incredible by any standard, and the cost of housing is going up at a rate of some 20 percent a year.

On the Island of Maui, recently, condominiums in a fashionable town were selling for $270,000. Two years before, the same apartments cost $90,000. Hawaii's land fever is converting. huge tracts of undeveloped land, some of it on the sides of still-active volcanoes, into new towns and resorts at a pace that would have amazed the easy-going Polynesians who were there before the white man came. The prices would have amazed the white men themselves. If you can find a vacation cottage for less than $50,000, buy it. It's a comparative steal.

Mainlanders, some of whom have never set foot on the islands, are buying building lots sight unseen for $2,000 an acre and more. The name of the game is speculation, even though much of the land is virtually useless because there is no water, nor any prospect of getting it there. Other investors find Hawaiian condominiums the answer to a dream. They buy a share in a development, which legally stays undivided and in the hands of an association set up to take care of the grounds and to generate more income by renting the units to vacationers. When the condominium owner goes to Hawaii for a meeting of the association, he deducts the cost of the trip from his income tax as a business expense!

It's a proposition that's hard to turn down, and it's become a challenge to the Hawaiian government. The cost of housing has gone well beyond the reach of many Hawaiians, and some have moved into run-down shanty towns that have none of the charm of the little grass shacks of their ancestors. But, like their ancestors, they have discovered that the best thing about being able to buy land is that you can also sell it. Almost any property owner there will tell you the government's effort to put limits on expansion is an idea whose time has come. But every new development scheme, and there are plenty of them, is an opportunity that puts a strain on the limits, and it's easy to say, "let's allow this one because it will bring new jobs for the people."

When Mark Twain arrived in Honolulu more than 100 years ago, he wrote: "The more I traveled through the town, the better I liked it. Every step revealed a new contrast. ...In place of the grand mud-colored brown fronts of San Francisco, I saw dwellings of straw, adobes and cream-colored pebble-and-shell conglomerated coral ...also a great number of neat white cottages, with green window shutters. In place of front yards like billiard tables with iron fences around them I saw these homes surrounded by ample yards, thickly clad with green grass and shaded by tall trees. ...In place of the customary geranium, calla lily, etc., languishing in dust and general debility, I saw luxurious banks and thickets of flowers, fresh as a meadow after a rain, and glowing with the richest dyes. In place of San Francisco's pleasure grove, the 'Willows,' I saw huge-bodied, wide-spreading forest trees with strange names and stranger appearance – trees that cast a shadow like a thundercloud and were able to stand alone without being tied to green poles.

"...I looked on a multitude of people, some white, in white coats, vests, pantaloons, even white cloth shoes, made snowy with chalk duly laid on every morning; but the majority of people were almost as dark as negroes – women with comely features, fine black eyes, rounded forms, inclining to the voluptuous, clad in a single red or white garment that fell free and unconfined from shoulder to heel, long black hair falling loose, gypsy hats encircled with wreaths of natural flowers of a brilliant carmine tint; plenty of dark men in various costumes, and some with nothing on but a battered stovepipe hat tilted on the nose, and a very scant breechclout. Certain children were clothed in nothing but sunshine – a very neat-fitting and picturesque apparel indeed.

"Instead of roughs and rowdies staring and blackguarding on the corners, I saw long-haired, saddle-colored Sandwich Island maidens sitting on the ground in the shade of corner houses. ...Instead of wretched cobblestone pavements, I walked in a firm foundation of coral, built up from the bottom of the sea by the absurd but persevering insect of that name, with a light layer of lava and cinders overlying (it).

"Instead of cramped and crowded streetcars, I met dusky native women sweeping by, free as the wind on fleet horses with gaudy riding sashes streaming like banners behind them.

"Instead of the combined stenches of Chinatown and Brannon Street slaughterhouses, I breathed the balmy fragrance of jessamine, oleander and the pride of India. In place of the hurry and bustle and noisy confusion of San Francisco, I moved in the midst of a summer calm as tranquil as dawn in the Garden of Eden. In place of the Golden City's skirting sand hills and the placid bay, I saw on one side a framework of tall, precipitous mountains close at hand, clad in refreshing green and cleft by deep, cool, chasmlike valleys. In front, the grand sweep of the ocean: a brilliant, transparent green near the shore, bound and bordered by a long white line of foamy spray dashing against the reef. Farther out, the dead water of the deep sea, flecked with whitecaps. In the far horizon, a single, lonely sail – a mere accent mark to emphasize a slumberous calm and solitude that were without a sound or limit. When the sun sunk down – the one intruder from other realms and persistent in suggestions of them – it was tranced luxury to sit in the perfumed air and forget that there was any world but these enchanted islands."

Mark Twain wouldn't recognize Honolulu today. But then, he wouldn't recognize San Francisco, either. The neat little buildings he saw have been replaced by something quite different, and today's travelers' first impression of the place is usually the long row of high-rise buildings on Waikiki beach. The city has now become a place of skyscrapers and souvenir shops, tour buses and the biggest resort hotels in the world. It's a bustling city with an ethnic mix that makes it different from almost any other city in the United States.

Honolulu is the capital city and its population reflects the mixture of people you'll find in all the islands. Less than half are haoles, Western whites; about a quarter are Japanese and about 15 percent are descended from the original Polynesians who were the first to arrive there. The balance of the population is Filipino, Chinese, Korean, Black and others.

It's an exotic blend that's sheer joy for people-watchers. The delicate features of the Japanese, the handsome faces of the Chinese, the legendary beauty of the Polynesians, add up to a spectacle that's hard to resist. Even the haole seem more beautiful here than anywhere else.

Downtown Honolulu today doesn't look much different from Houston or any other American city that has gone through a building boom in the last twenty years. But don't let that fool you. There is a difference! Sure, Kalakaua Avenue, like main streets in other parts of the country, has been converted to a car-less shopping mall. The convention halls and continental restaurants are air-conditioned. And you stand a good chance of meeting someone from your home town when you go there on a vacation.

You begin to notice the difference when you sit on a terrace overlooking the Pacific and you're served local pineapple or papaya for breakfast. You see it in the side streets, or in a Chinese cemetery where families feed their dead and keep them contented. You hear it in the streets, where the old Hawaiian songs still haunt the air. You get a sense of the past in Honolulu's Bishop Museum, founded as a memorial to a Hawaiian princess who married a New Englander at 18. Mrs. Bishop was heiress to the lands and treasures of the Kamehameha family, and these treasures form the nucleus of the museum's collection. The old royal thrones and crowns are here, along with a rare collection of feathered adornments made for the chiefs and kings of old Hawaii. The rich colors and design of the cloaks impressed Captain Cook, who noted in his journal that "...even in countries where dress is more attended to, (they) might be reckoned elegant. The ground of them is a net-work upon which the most beautiful red and yellow feathers are so closely fixed that the surface might be compared to the thickest and richest velvet."

The Bishop Museum also has a planetarium, reflecting an interest in the stars that goes back to the earliest times. Today, one of the world's most important astronomical observatories is on the Island of Hawaii, at the top of Mount Mauna Kea. The summit of the volcano is at an altitude of almost 14,000 feet, so high that clouds rarely pass over it, and astronomers feel it is the best place in the northern hemisphere for looking out into the universe.

The Island of Oahu, where Honolulu is located, is relatively small, and can be explored easily. It's ringed by beaches, the most famous of which is Waikiki. The Hawaiian royalty reserved Waikiki for themselves, but the Hawaiians of today have generally turned it over to the tourists. They go to Ala Moana Beach, not far away, for swimming and tanning. When it's surfing they want, they load their surfboards on their cars and head north to Makaha, or another of the "big surf" beaches across the island. For snorkeling, they go to the underwater sanctuary at Hanauma Bay. For privacy, they pass the "blowhole," a dramatic geyser that erupts every time the waves hit a hole in the lava ledge, sending a huge waterspout into the air, to get to Halona Cove, a small beach hidden away between the cliffs.

Diamond Head, an extinct volcano, is also on the Island of Oahu. You can go inside the crater and have a look around, if you like. The old Hawaiians called it heahi, which means "the place of fire." It got a new name from British sailors who thought they had found diamonds there. What they really found were volcanic crystals.

Visitors to Oahu can get a glimpse of Samoa and Tahiti, New Zealand or Fiji by visiting the Polynesian Cultural Center. It's a collection of villages of the kind that would be found on the other islands with a Polynesian tradition. Young Polynesians work their way through college by demonstrating the old ways of life, singing and dancing in authentic native costume. Old Hawaii is there, too, in a village of triangular houses covered in pili grass ...the famous "little grass shacks" you often hear about, but don't see much in Hawaii these days.

There's a bird sanctuary on Oahu, too. It's called Paradise Park (there's that word again!). There are also 15 golf courses, 90 tennis courts, 50 miles of beaches and 600 places to go surfing. And just so you don't get homesick, it has Ala Moana Shopping Center, one of the biggest in the world. Most of the hotels have their own shopping malls, too. In fact, about the only thing that makes the hotels of Oahu different from those you'd find in any American city with palm trees and a beach is that every one of them offers church services every Sunday morning in their schedule of activities. It's just one more way the influence of the missionaries hangs on.

Pearl Harbor, named for the pearl oysters that once thrived there, is part of the Oahu scene. The Hawaiians believed this was originally the home of Kaahupahua, the queen of the sharks. She lived, they said, in a cavern that was a majestic palace guarded by a brother shark. She protected the people by decreeing that sharks should not molest humans, and she backed her decree with an order to her shark people to be constantly on the alert to kill any man-eaters that might invade the waters near the island.

When the U.S. Navy began dredging the channel to open Pearl Harbor in 1900, they were warned by the Hawaiians that they were risking the wrath of both the gods and the sharks. To avoid it, they carefully removed a shrine that had been built in their path and took it, stone-by-stone, out to sea, where it was lowered carefully to the ocean floor in a reverent ceremony.

The jumbo jets deliver tourists hundreds at a time to Honolulu airport. If they're from New York, they've been on the plane for 13 hours and they've had to push their watches ahead another six hours. Or, if they prefer to be on real Hawaiian time, they take their watches off. Radio and television stations are about the only institutions in the Islands that follow anything like a strict time schedule, and even they occasionally forget. There's a carillon in Waikiki that plays Hawaiian tunes as it strikes the hour, but the music rarely begins until the hour is at least 10 minutes old.

Most of the mainlanders and others who pass through the airport stay right on Oahu, but there is great enthusiasm building for the other islands. Many visitors hop a hydrofoil to go 22 miles east to Molokai, the one they call "the friendly isle." Still a little off the beaten path, it manages to keep some of the the the character of the old Hawaii. For many years, it has been the site of a treatment center for leprosy. The colony at Kalaupapa was taken over by a Belgian priest, Father Joseph Damien de Veuster, in 1873. He found sub-human conditions there, and gave his life to building the settlement into a place of dignity and hope. The colony is still there, a memorial to Father Damien, the "Martyr of Molokai."

Molokai was slow to grow because water was scarce there. But it's plentiful in the mountains on the northern side, and the combination of lush forests and towering cliffs, some as high as 3,600 feet, make if the most majestically beautiful of all the islands. Fishing is great there, too. A shelf of land extends more than 25 miles out from the island, making one of the richest fishing grounds in all of Hawaii. You'll find deer in the forests, too. They were put there in 1869 by the Duke of Edinburgh, who received them as a gift from the Emperor of Japan.

There are huge pineapple plantations on Molokai, and cattle ranches, too. King Kamehameha V himself raised longhorns out here in the 1860s. When he wasn't rasslin' steers, he found time to plant a grove of 1,000 coconut trees on ten acres just outside Kaunakakai, the island's main town.

Just beyond Molokai is Lanai, the "Pineapple Island." It's owned by Castle & Cook, a company most people know because of a company it owns, the Dole Company. They bought this island, 18 by 13 miles wide, back in 1922 for $1,100,000. They built a company town there and transformed the island into a huge pineapple plantation with good roads, a deep-water port, camp grounds and a casual mountain hotel with fireplaces in the rooms.

Naturally, just about everybody on Lanai works for the pineapple company, but the shops, service stations, theaters and such are all privately owned. The old natives say that Lanai was, for a thousand years, the home of evil spirits. An exile from Maui named Kaulalaau got rid of them and made it safe for human habitation, just like Saint Patrick did for Ireland. That was all many, many years ago, obviously, because archaeologists have found one of the best-preserved Hawaiian ruins in the islands of Kaunola, which was also a favorite fishing spot of Kamehameha the Great.

Lanai is also a paradise for hunters. It abounds in pronghorn antelope, partridge, pheasant and wild goats. In some parts of the island the season is open all the year for bow and arrow hunting.

Captain Vancouver, a British explorer who followed Captain Cook to the islands, described Lanai as a "naked island which seemed thinly covered with shriveled grass in a scorched state." He wouldn't recognize it today! Today, hikers stroll through forests of Norfolk pine, and the more than 13,000 acres of pineapple trees are in anything but a "scorched state."

For years, the "in" crowd, film stars and the like, have been going to the island of Maui, which is quite different from all the others. It was created by two big volcanoes that formed two mountain masses joined together by a thin strip of land. The strip of land is where you'll find most of the hotels and condominiums that make this the second most popular tourist island in Hawaii. One of the things they go there to see is Haleakala, the largest dormant volcano in the world. And it's worth the trip! The mountain is more than 10,000 feet high and the crater is 21 miles around. Inside it are caverns, a lake, meadows, forests, even a desert, and the biggest raspberry bushes you've ever seen.

Maui was a favorite stop for the whaling ships that passed by in the late 19th century. The seaport town of Lahaina was a lively place back then, with sailors fighting over the girls who swam out to meet their ships, or drawing knives and belaying pins just for the fun of it.

Finally the whalers all went home, and sugar cane took over, which wasn't nearly as much fun for anybody. But it was quieter, and that made it attractive to tourists, which has now made Lahaina a lively town again. And the trip from the main town of Wailuku is breathtakingly beautiful. They've recreated the flavor of the old whaling town there, and though you're not likely to get hit on the head with a belaying pin, you'll find it a fascinating trip into the past. The annual Whaling Spree, a yacht race to Honolulu held in the fall, usually begins on the verandah of the Old Whaler's Grog Shop at the Pioneer Inn, a waterfront landmark, and possibly one of Maui's most popular spots. Just about five miles from it, the Kaanapali Coast is quickly becoming one of the most popular spots in all the islands. It has beautiful beaches on one side and majestic mountains on the other. But if that's not enough for pleasure-seeking travelers (and it rarely seems to be), the hand of man has added a couple of golf courses, a string of first-rate hotels and an airport that makes getting there simple. It even has a shopping center to keep the traveler from getting too homesick.

People who prefer natural beauty in its natural state find it on Kauai, probably the most relaxed of any of the islands. When people who make movies or television commercials are looking for an idyllic setting, they always wind up on Kauai.

The natives call it the "garden island," but its landscape includes some awesome cliffs and rugged canyons along with the brightly-colored flowers and lush trees that spill over into the water at the edge of smooth, sandy beaches. The beaches are nearly deserted most of the time, and inland you could spend hours wandering through quiet valleys and not see another soul.

Archaeologists have found remains of a culture that seems to have thrived in Kauai long before the Polynesians came. The Polynesians themselves have legends about it. They called them the "Menehune," and said they were a race of elflike creatures not more than three feet tall, capable of complex engineering feats like changing the course of rivers or damming them up to make better fishing holes. They worked only at night, of course, so not many people ever got to actually see them. But every once in a while somebody strolling in the moonlight near one of Kauai's spectacular waterfalls sees one of the little people hurrying by. Sightings are rare, but people who live there can show you plenty of examples of their work.

Photographers can't get enough of Kauai. Wainea Canyon is a place they adore because the look of it alters from hour to hour as the light changes. The Wailua River, once considered so sacred it didn't have a name lest someone should be tempted to talk about it, is the scene of several ancient temples. One of them was called a "temple of refuge," placed there as a sanctuary where someone who had broken a tabu or had been defeated in battle could be guaranteed safety. But there was a catch: the transgressor had to get there ahead of the people who were chasing him.

One of Hawaii's most fascinating resort hotels, Coco Palms, is on Kauai. It was built to conform to the old traditions and to recreate as many of them as possible. Every evening at dusk, a group of young men sound a note on conch shells, first in the direction of the mountains, then toward the sea. It's an ancient signal to everyone within earshot that "the drums will talk." As they finish, the drums do talk in a beat that announces that a feast has been prepared. And that, in turn, signals the lighting of torches in the hotel's 30-acre palm grove.

The site of the hotel is the royal grove of the old Kauai kings, and the Coco Palms has a museum with mementos of the royalty who once played there.

There's a spectacular waterspout on this island, too. When the surf hits a hole in the rock called "Spouting Horn," it sends a jet of water 100 feet into the air. And when that happens, you can hear what sounds like a deep sigh from another hole nearby. It's the sound, the natives say, of a dragon who swam in there centuries ago and can't find its way out.

Less than 20 miles, but hundreds of years, away is the tiny island of Niihau. According to legend, no one may ever visit there, and if a Hawaiian leaves, he is forbidden to return. It's not quite true. Visitors are allowed to go to Niihau, but only invited guests. And Hawaiians who leave are welcomed back. But not many ever leave, because they like it there.

A century ago, Elizabeth Sinclair, a Scottish

woman from New Zealand, having lost her husband, packed all her belongings and her children and grandchildren into a small boat and set out for Canada. She stopped off in Honolulu, where she met King Kamehameha IV. He was so charmed by her that he offered to give her some land nearby. She had cattle ranching on her mind, and so refused the offer and sailed on. She went to Vancouver, but didn't like what she found there, so she loaded up the schooner again and went back to Hawaii.

She paid the king $10,000 for the 72-square mile island of Niihau, and got some coastal land on Kauai in the bargain. Her son-in-law, a man named Robinson, became the lord of the island, and when he died over 30 years ago, his widow and five children became the sole owners of Niihau.

There are 300 people living there now, all pure-blooded Hawaiians, all speaking the pure, unadulterated language of their forefathers. There are public schools, and the children are taught English. But none of them takes it too seriously. There aren't any dogs, policemen or even movies on Niihau. During World War II, when, incidentally, they had an uninvited guest in the form of a Japanese pilot who crash-landed there, radios were introduced by the U.S. Army Signal Corps. Today, all the people who live there are crazy about radios. And recently the government, with the kind of wisdom governments everywhere are so fond of showing, has sent them battery-powered TV sets.

For years, the islanders earned their living by raising cattle and sheep and keeping bees. The cost of transporting cattle from the island to the marketplace has put them out of that business. And the low prices paid for wool took all the profit out of raising sheep. Today they earn their keep by making grass mats, leis and other handicrafts for sale in Honolulu.

In spite of the intrusion of TV sets and newspapers and other trappings of the 20th century, Niihau is one of the last places on earth where simple, feudal life still exists. It's the only place where old Hawaii still lives.

There are other islands in Hawaii that tourists never see. Kahoolawe is used for target practice by the U.S. military, and visiting there would surely be dangerous to your health. Lehua and Molokini as well as Kuala are all barren rocks sitting there like the Ancient Mariner, surrounded by water without a drop to drink.

There are many barren spots in this paradise they call Hawaii. In fact, with 49 other states to choose from, NASA picked Hawaii as the place best suited to give the Apollo astronauts a good idea of what they'd find when they went to the moon. It's not all dry, of course. The wettest spot in the world is a mountain top in Kauai that gets an average of **40 feet** of rain a year. In 1948, they got 624.1 inches of rain up there ...a little more than 52 feet!

But Hawaii is mainly gentle breezes and bright sunshine, and that's why people go there. A lot of people go there to watch the sun set because it probably doesn't set as beautifully anywhere in the world as it does on the Kona Coast, on the big island that gave all the islands its name, Hawaii. The huge volcano Mauna Loa keeps the wind away from the coast, and every morning it's bright and sunny there because the clouds can't get over the mountain. They often win the battle by the middle of the day, and when they do, they act like an umbrella that keeps the hot sun off the beach and the temperature down. Combined with the rich soil of the volcano, it makes a perfect atmosphere for growing coffee, and plenty of it is grown there. In fact, Hawaii is the only place in the United States where you'll find coffee plantations. Kamehameha I and his chiefs used the Kona Coast as their principal playground. The king spent his last years there, fishing for the fabulous game fish, including the Pacific blue marlin. But, when they were all younger, they didn't think anything in the world was more fun than holua ...toboganning down the side of a snowless mountain. The remains of one of their runs is still there – a slide about a mile long on a hillside. They had it covered with grass cuttings and had themselves a ball!

One of the biggest cattle ranches in the United States is right near the Kona Coast. The Parker Ranch has been growing since a New Englander, John Palmer Parker, gave up the life of a sailor to become a cowboy in 1847. His spread was no threat to the big guys who were getting established in the American Southwest at the time. It was only two acres. It's grown today to well over a quarter of a million acres. And it has the big advantage over its Texas competitors of that wonderful Hawaiian seacoast. And those sunsets!

Most of the beaches on the islands are made of fine white sand that feels terrific underfoot. It feels so good, in fact, that the missionaries, persuasive as they were, were never able to talk the Hawaiian people into wearing shoes. Even today, the islands aren't exactly a paradise for shoe salesmen. On the big island of Hawaii, that fine white sand comes in a variety of colors, including green at one point. But the most unusual is on the southern coast, where the beaches and sand dunes are black.

This coast is the traditional home of the fire goddess, Pele, and the black sand is just one example of her work. Another is the island itself, which is more than twice as big as all the other islands put together. And it's getting bigger because Pele is still at it. She breathes fire through the huge Mauna Loa volcano, and sometimes, when the mood strikes her, she makes Kilauea boil over. The territory around the mountains, now a national park, is an experience no one ever forgets. The black beaches and sand dunes, made of pulverized lava, are just the beginning. Going into Hawaii Volcanoes National Park is like going into another world. Thousands of acres are covered with cinders and a crust of lava that has been hardened into patterns that look like a pan of molasses that's been neglected. There's a whole forest of the ghosts of trees whose roots were sealed off by a lava flow; and another living forest that was left undisturbed when a lava river forked around a 100-acre space to form a green island in the midst of the desolation. There's a hotel and a golf course in the park, in probably the most unusual setting for either one anywhere in the world.

But what makes the park truly unique is Mauna Loa and Kilauea, both very much alive. It's possible to get to the top of Mauna Loa and look into its awesome fire pit. But getting there isn't half the fun. There's a paved road about halfway up the side of the mountain, but after that, it's an 18-mile hike to the summit. Hardy hikers say the trip is worth it, but most people prefer to take their word for it. And after all, there's another volcano right next door, and it's spectacular too.

Kilauea also has the advantages of being easier to climb. The trip to the top is 9,000 feet shorter and, with a little bit of luck, people who take the trip see volcanic activity inside the crater, even an occasional eruption. Every once in a while, somebody reports seeing Pele herself. She's beautiful and still young, they say, with long, flowing red hair. Sometimes she even talks to them to explain where the next river of fiery lava will go.

When that occurs, there's no guarantee it will actually happen that way; Pele has been known to change her mind.

Most people drive around the rim in their cars. There is an observation platform on the brink of it, giving an unforgettable view of the fire pit inside. The pit is like a big kettle about a half-mile around and about 750 feet deep. That's where the spectacular fire fountains and melted lava come from. Most of the time, the lava stays inside the crater, but now and then Pele decides to put on a show and the whole thing spills over. When it does, the island grows a little more.

Every now and then, nature takes a little away from the big island. Huge tidal waves, which the natives call *tsunamis*, have come roaring across the Pacific, even in recent times, to bring havoc to the island's main city, Hilo. Every time one has hit, Hilo has hit back, moving a little bit farther inland and putting up bigger and better breakwaters against the next tsunami.

They're a tough bunch, these Hawaiians. Nothing keeps them down for long. They endure volcanoes, tidal waves, tourist invasions, even missionaries, with good-humored charm. They'll jump at any excuse for a good party, and the best idea for a party in any of the 50 states is an authentic Hawaiian luau.

Today luaus are staple fare at most of the big hotels, and you'll find everybody from the Hauloowoona chapter of Hadassah to the friendly sons of Polynesia sponsoring them for profit as well as for fun. In the beginning, the luau was the big event in small villages, a tradition similar to New England clambakes. The name itself means "taro leaf," which the old-timers used for food. Their parties were held in the center of the villages, and everybody in town was invited ...indeed, everybody in town helped prepare it. The setting, lit by festive torches, included the dazzling flowers and tropical foliage that sets the scene for so much of the charm of the islands.

It took the whole day to get a good luau together. First the men dug a huge pit and lined it with rocks. Then they built a fire to heat the rocks. Next, they split a pig open, filled it with heated rocks and wrapped it in taro leaves. The pig was buried in the pit and left to roast most of the day. By the time it was ready to eat, it was the best-tasting roast pork any culture ever devised.

But man cannot live by pork alone. Not at a luau. The bill of fare included roast chicken, laulau – a piece of pork wrapped together with salmon and roasted – baked yams with pineapple, shredded salmon mixed with fresh tomatoes and onions and eaten raw, and steamed taro leaves. Poi was included, too, served with dried seaweed. And for desert, coconut cream pudding, called noupio.

When there was nothing special to celebrate, the average Hawaiian lived on poi, the mainstay of the diet in the islands for longer than anyone can remember. Mark Twain described it as something that looks like "...common flour paste, kept in large bowls formed of species of gourd and capable of holding from one to three or four gallons. Poi is prepared from the taro plant ...when boiled, it answers as a passable substitute for bread. The buck Kanakas bake it underground, then mash it with a heavy lava pestle, mix water with it until it becomes a paste, set it aside and let it ferment, and then it is poi – and an unseductive mixture it is, almost tasteless before it ferments and too sour for a luxury afterward. But nothing is more nutritious. When solely used, however, it produces acrid humors, a fact which sufficiently accounts for the humorous character of the kanakas. I think there must be as much of a knack in handling poi as there is in eating with chopsticks. The forefinger is thrust into the mess and stirred quickly round several times and drawn as quickly out, thickly coated, just as if it were poulticed; the head is thrown back, the finger inserted in the mouth, and the delicacy stripped off and swallowed – the eye closing gently, meanwhile, in a languid sort of ecstasy. Many a different finger goes into the same bowl and many a different kind of dirt and shade and quality of flavor is added to the virtues of its contents."

If Mark Twain was implying that eating native food in Hawaii is bad for your health, don't believe it! Hawaiians are the healthiest people in the United States. Life expectancy in the U.S. is just under 73 years at this point. The average Hawaiian can expect to live almost 76 years. Hawaiian women, with the longest life span of any American, average almost 78 years. Hawaiian women almost never die in childbirth, and heart disease, cancer and stroke kill far fewer in Hawaii than anywhere else in the country. Of course, with that climate, they don't get pneumonia of flu very often, either. And to top it all, the ratio of doctors to the population is among America's highest, even though there isn't much for any of them to do, apparently.

It isn't clear whether the "Aloha Spirit" keeps them alive or whether they stay around longer to enjoy the "Aloha Spirit." But that spirit is something that makes Hawaii unique among the 50 states.

It's a combination of remembering history and respecting tradition. It's taking joy from beauty and honoring grace. It's taking paradise seriously.

Hawaiians do all those things. Their life is generally joyful, and joy is like a contagious disease ...as anyone who has ever been close to it knows very well.

The easternmost tip of Hawaii Island is the Puna District, an area rich in geological wonders and wild, beautiful seascapes. Top: Black Sand Beach, at Kaimu, which is formed by tiny volcanic particles and visited by great Pacific waves that are ideal for surfers (above). Facing page: (top) the spray-washed coastline of Opihikao. (Bottom) resembling some man-made monument, strange columns of lava stand in a forest once engulfed by a lava flow.

Previous pages left: the dramatic Na Ulu Sea Arches. Left: bright red anthurium blooms, which thrive in the shade of the giant tree ferns around Pahoa, on Hawaii Island. Until Mount St. Helens became active, Volcanoes National Park (remaining pictures) contained America's only two live volcanoes. One of these, Kilauea Iki, last erupted in 1959, sending fountains of red lava 1,900 feet into the air. Today, molten lava still bubbles beneath the surface of its vast crater (previous page right and top). Above: amaumau ferns growing near the crater of the formidable Halemaumau Firepit, which last erupted in 1974, and (facing page) the blackened southwest rift zone.

Previous pages: Devastation Trail in Hawaii Island's Volcanoes National Park (these pages). The effects of the 1959 eruption of Kilauea can be seen in this eerie landscape of black pumice, littered with the skeleton-like remains of ohia trees. Facing page: (top and bottom right) the steaming Sulphur Banks, and (bottom left) an offering left for the volcano goddess, Pele, at her home, the smoking Halemaumau Firepit. Top: young ferns grow amid a jumble of *aa*, the form of lava that solidifies into small, rough rocks, and (above and right) rare plants and flowers bring occasional splashes of color to the gray and brown wasteland of Devastation Trail.

Facing page: (top) Devastation Trail, where a wooden boardwalk crosses the blackened landscape for half a mile, and (bottom) steaming sulphur gases rising from the Halemaumau Firepit. Situated within the 2.5-mile-long, 2-mile-wide crater of Kilauea volcano, the firepit was, for over a century, a bubbling, sometimes overflowing, lava lake. Then, with the steam explosion of 1924, its diameter more than doubled, leaving a hole some 1,300 feet deep. Inside the firepit lava still boils away at around 2,000 degrees Fahrenheit. Above: a forest of giant tree ferns and ohia trees near the Thurston Lava Tube, all in Hawaii Island's Volcanoes National Park.

Facing page: (top pictures) a Hawaiian girl and children await the arrival of disembarking passengers in order to proffer the traditional garlands or *leis*, (bottom) flower-bedecked crewmen on the U.S.S. Beaufort, and (right) a Japanese training ship, all at Hilo Harbor. Hilo, Hawaii Island's only city, sprawls alongside the crescent-shaped bay that gave it its name, which means new moon. Once a sleepy little sugar cane town, it is now an important financial and shipping center, its harbor busy with ships and tankers from all over the world. Languishing in the great arc of Hilo Bay is palm-fringed Coconut Island (above), a pleasant picnic spot offering fine views of the leafy city across the water.

海王丸 東京

Among the sensuous images associated with Hawaii Island are the brilliant colors of rare and beautiful flowers, each with its own heady fragrance. Sometimes called Orchid Island, it boasts over 20,000 varieties of orchids, as well as richly-colored anthuriums and other tropical plants. Top and above: plumeria, which comes in many varieties and is used for making garlands or *leis*, (left) the delicate and complex blooms of the phalaenopsis roselle, and (facing page) one of the more common types of orchid found on the island.

The many exquisite flowers found on Hawaii Island include (top and above) varieties of Vanda orchid, (top left) an unusual ixora, a relative of the coffee plant, (left) phalaenopsis schillerana, (facing page) water hyacinth, and (center left) Cattleya orchids, which were named after the 18th-century horticulturalist William Cattley, who found them being used as packing material and nurtured them for six years until they bloomed.

Previous pages: (right) the Akaka Falls, in the magnificent arboretum of Akaka Falls State Park (left) near Hilo (these pages), on Hawaii Island. Above: pagodas, bridges and stone lanterns contribute to the oriental beauty of the Liliuokalani Gardens, on the Waiakea Peninsula. Top: Wailuku River State Park, the site of Rainbow Falls (facing page top), where at sunrise, in the mist at the base of the falls, a rainbow is formed. Facing page bottom: a sea view from the scenic route by the Botanical Gardens.

Facing page: the Kolekole Stream tumbles over rocky steps and (above) cascades over the 442-foot-high precipice of Akaka Falls, in Akaka Falls State Park. Covering 66 acres with varieties of giant ferns, azaleas, orchids, gingers and bamboo, this lush park is one of the spectacles of the beautiful Hamakua Coast Drive between Hilo and Kailua-Kona. Another is the Laupahoehoe Beach Park area (overleaf), where jagged black lava rocks rise out of a sapphire sea. Despite its beauty, however, this park is haunted by echoes of tragedy, for in 1946 it was hit by a tidal wave that took the lives of 24 students and teachers.

The 90-mile-long Hamakua Coast Drive passes near some of the finest of Hawaii Island's many beauty spots, including (top) the silvery waterfall and rugged cliffs at Maulua Gulch, near Weloka, (right) the spectacular Akaka Falls, in Akaka Falls State Park, (facing page) the grassy peninsula of Laupahoehoe Beach Park, and (above and overleaf) the remarkable Waipio Valley, a great gap in the windward side of the Kohala Mountains. Overlooked by 2,000-foot-high cliffs, a stream meanders gently along the valley floor, which is colored by a patchwork of taro fields. It was in this magnificent setting, in 1780, that Kamehameha was elected by reigning chiefs as Hawaii's ruler, thus beginning the Great Dynasty.

In 1809, a young ex-seaman, John Palmer Parker, was hired by Kamehameha I to round up wild, stray cattle. By 1815 he had domesticated them and established a small ranch. Today it is one of the most extensive private ranches in America and runs the world's largest herd of Hereford cattle. Top right: cattle pens in the ranch country around Waimea, where the Parker Ranch (above and top left) covers about 250,000 acres of pastureland on the slopes of Mauna Kea and the Kohala Mountains. Facing page: (top) a view from the Pololu Valley lookout near Niulii, on Hawaii Island's northeast coast, and (bottom) lava rocks and white pebbles on the beach of Lapakahi State Historic Park, on the northwest coast.

In the late 1800s, the Hawaiian Legislature commissioned a statue of Kamehameha I to be placed in Honolulu. A fine gilt and bronze monument was sculpted in Italy by an American, Thomas R. Gould, but it was lost at sea en route to Hawaii. Gould made another, which two years later was erected in Honolulu. However, only a few weeks after the replica's unveiling, the original appeared at the city's harbor, having been salvaged from the depths of the sea. It was this statue (right), the more lifelike of the two effigies, that was placed in Kapuua, on Hawaii Island's Kohala Coast - the birthplace of Kamehameha. Many believe it was always destined to be there. Top: a home near Waimea, (above) a ranch by the Hamakua Coast, and (facing page) cinder cones on Mauna Kea.

Previous pages: (left bottom) the Mauna Kea Beach Golf Course, and (remaining pictures) the idyllic, crescent-shaped beach of the Mauna Kea Beach Hotel, on Hawaii Island's sunny South Kohala Coast. This area, together with the Kona Coast, further south, forms a region combining luxury modern resorts with remnants of old Hawaii. Kailua, the Kona Coast's main town, has many interesting historic attractions, including (top) Hawaii's oldest church, the Mokuaikaua Church, and the gracious Hulihee Palace, both built in the 1830s. Right: one of the crew of Captain Bean's Royal Polynesian Canoe (above), in Kailua Bay, and (facing page) weighing the marlin catch on Kailua Pier.

A spectacular golf course (above), surrounded by lava-covered fields, and an inviting swimming pool (facing page) are just two of the attractive features of the Mauna Lani Bay Hotel (top). One of the most luxurious resort hotels on Hawaii Island's South Kohala Coast, it is worth around $70 million, each of its 351 rooms having been built at an average cost of $200,000. Right and overleaf: palm trees shade tiny St. Peter's Catholic Church, which was built on the site of an ancient Hawaiian temple on the Kona Coast's beautiful Kahaluu Bay.

Top left: the picturesque Kauahaao Congregational Church in the litte town of Waiohinu, in southern Hawaii Island, (top) the speckled lava beach of Milolii, a small fishing village on the Kona Coast, (above) strange formations of *pahoehoe* lava, and (left) the interior of St. Benedict's Catholic Church, or the Painted Church. Situated inland from the Kona Coast, near Honaunau, and decorated with ornate murals and Hawaiian motifs, the church is a masterpiece of folk art. This area is also the site of the famous City of Refuge (facing page), a reconstruction of the sacred sanctuary which for 400 years provided a safe haven for lawbreakers, defeated warriors and noncombatants.

When ancient Hawaiians broke sacred laws, it was believed that the gods would retaliate with violent acts, such as volcanic eruptions and tidal waves. Thus lawbreakers were swiftly executed by the anxious community, unless they could reach a sanctuary, where they could be absolved by a priest. The City of Refuge at Honaunau Bay, on the Kona Coast is one of the most historic of these sanctuaries. Destroyed by Christian Hawaiians in 1829, the site was made a National Historic Park in 1961 and reconstruction of the city was begun. It now includes the remarkable wooden images of gods standing on guard by the thatched temple of Hale-o-Keawe (these pages).

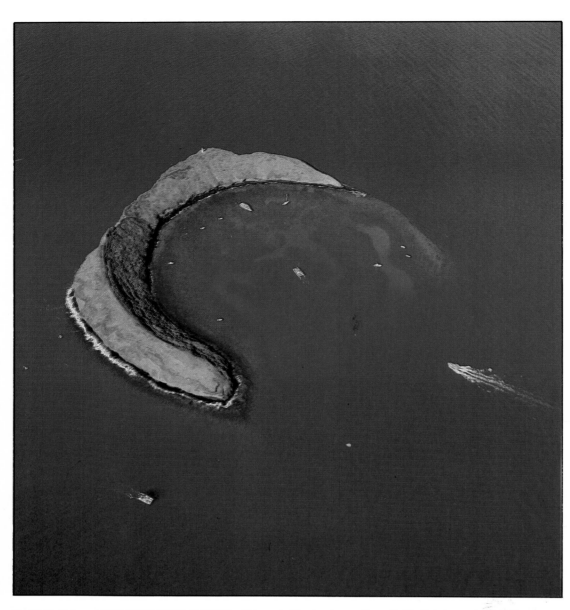

Tiny, crescent-shaped Molokini Island (left) is primarily known for its superb snorkeling waters, although some traditional Hawaiians still respect it as the home of ancestral spirits. It is located off the west coast of Maui, the second largest of Hawaii's six islands. Created by two volcanoes that flowed together to form a low plateau between them, Maui is often known as the Valley Isle. One of its volcanoes is the famous Haleakala, or House of the Sun, the largest dormant volcano in the world. Below: sunset seen from Haleakala Highway. Facing page: (top) yellow poppies adorn the eerie landscape of the dryland forest around the Piilani Highway, by Kanaio in southern Maui, and (bottom) the view west from Highway 377, towards the sea and the cloud-kissed West Maui Mountains.

Previous pages: (left bottom) one of the stunning views from the 10,023-foot-high summit of Mount Haleakala, which dominates the island of Maui. Surrounded by the 20,000 acres of Haleakala National Park, this great dormant volcano is the most visited attraction on the island. Inside its vast, 21-mile-circumference crater (remaining pictures) is a lunar-like landscape of rich and ever-changing colors, comprising meadows, valleys, caverns, nine cinder cones, and such strange and wonderful plants as the rare silversword (above), which blossoms only once in its lifetime of up to twenty years. Amongst the other exotic plants to be found on Maui are (facing page top) the bird of paradise flower, which originates from southern Africa, (facing page bottom) plumeria, and (right) dwarf poinciana, named after M. de Poinci, a governor of the French West Indies.

Seven Pools (previous pages), or the Oheo Gulch as it is properly called, is one of the main attractions of the coastal section of Haleakala National Park, near Hana. Here, cool blue water tumbles through seven large pools, as well as several smaller ones, before reaching the sea. Also on the east coast of Maui is fascinating Waianapanapa State Park (these pages), where, amid lush and varied vegetation, are two great lava tubes filled with water, the eerie Waianapanapa and Waiomao caves. The coast here has a strange, rugged beauty, especially at Honokalani black sand beach (facing page bottom), which is washed by the waters of Pailoa Bay.

The Hana Highway runs for over 50 miles along the north coast of Maui, providing access to a variety of beauty spots, including the lovely Haipuaena Falls (previous pages left) near Keanae. As the road winds high above the sea towards this area the idyllic, unspoilt scenery of the Keanae Peninsula is spread out below, giving a glimpse of the Hawaii of bygone years. Here, patchwork patterns of green taro fields (previous pages right) are dotted with groves of swaying banana trees and coco palms. The blue Pacific turns to white foam at the rugged, lava coastline of this region (below and facing page), while further inland (left) sugar plantations cover the flat floor of Keanae Valley.

One of the finest of Hawaii's volcanic wonders is the spectacular
Iao Needle (these pages) in western Maui. Green as an emerald, with
its leafy covering, the 2,250-foot-high needle rises sharply from
the floor of the deep valley where, in 1790, King Kamehameha I
trapped and defeated the Maui army. The bodies of these warriors
choked the Iao Stream that cuts through the gorge, so the battle
was named Kepaniwai, meaning "the damming of the waters."

Overlooked by the green-mantled West Maui Mountains around the Iao Valley are the lovely Kepaniwai Heritage Gardens (previous pages), which were designed by landscape architect Richard C. Tongg. Here, pavilions and ornamental gardens reflect the various cultures of ethnic groups, including Japanese, Filipino and Chinese, that have been crucial to Hawaii's development. Left: sugar plantations in the Keanae Valley, (top) sunset over Kahului Bay, on the northern coast of the seven-mile-wide isthmus between West and East Maui, (facing page top) patches of light and shade dramatizing a view of the West Maui Mountains and richly-colored cane fields, and (facing page bottom) Kahakuloa Head, on West Maui's northeastern coastline. Overleaf: the sea turns from sunset gold to twilight silver at Wahikuli State Wayside Park, one of the perfect beaches along the white-sanded shoreline north of Lahaina.

Left: sails against a burnished sky create a timeless seascape at Wahikuli State Wayside Park (top), on Maui's westernmost shores. Further north, near Kahana, luxury resort hotels overlook golden sands washed by a sapphire sea (facing page top). On the island's most northerly coast is Mokuleia Bay (above) near Honolua, and the aptly-named Pineapple Hill (facing page bottom), where fields of these glossy green plants stretch down to the shores of the Pailolo Channel, across which can be seen the island of Molokai. Overleaf: (left top) an unforgettable Maui sunset, and (right) the west coast at Kaanapali, from which the island of Lanai (left bottom) is clearly visible.

During the mid-1800s, the fascinating town of Lahaina (these pages) became a busy whaling port visited by hordes of boisterous sailors, and it has retained much of the charm and the architecture of those days. Above: the Pioneer Inn, which dates from 1901 and contains relics of the whaling days, (left) a luxury beachside hotel, and (top) a catch of Marlin being laid out on the quayside. Facing page: (top) the *Carthaginian II*, a typical 19th-century brig now containing the "World of the Whale" exhibition, and (bottom) the beautifully-restored 1890s Sugar Cane Train, which now offers tours between Kaanapali and Lahaina, following much of the original track used by the Pioneer Sugar Mill.

Previous pages: (left top) Whalers Village, at Kaanapali, near Lahaina in West Maui. This unusual shopping center, with its picturesque oceanfront setting (remaining pictures), doubles as an open-air whaling museum, featuring such exhibits as a forty-foot-long whale skeleton. The soft contours of the great West Maui Mountains form a dramatic backdrop to Lahaina's colorful harbor (top and facing page top) and sugar cane fields (above) off the Hono a Pi'ilani Highway. Left: the giant, bronze Buddha, at the Lahaina Jodo Mission, which commemorates the arrival of the first Japanese immigrants in 1868. Facing page bottom: the Hana Highway, near Kaumahina State Wayside Park, in East Maui.

Now known as "the Friendly Isle," beautiful Molokai used to be shunned as "the Lonely Isle" due to the leper colony that was established in one of its most scenic areas in 1866. The virtually treeless, windswept Kalaupapa Peninsula (above), cut off from the rest of the island by great 2,000-foot-high cliffs, was once the isolated place where the tragic victims were cast and left to fend for themselves. Today, Kaluapapa is the site of the Hansen's Disease Leprosy Treatment Center, where less than 100 fully-cured patients choose to stay. No new patients have been admitted and it is, today, far more a monument to man's victory over disease than a place of suffering and death. This has contributed greatly to the changed image of Molokai and the island is increasingly appreciated for its natural beauty. Tourists are lured by experiences such as the view from the Kalaupapa Peninsula Overlook (facing page top) and the magnificent Pali Coast (remaining pictures), which can only be seen from a boat or helicopter. Stretching between Kalaupapa and the Halawa Valley, Pali's velvety, 200-foot-high cliffs, cut by the mouths of deep valleys and sprinkled with silver waterfalls, create one of the world's most magnificent coastlines.

Previous pages: a lush forest by the Kalaupapa Peninsula Overlook. These pages: the green Halawa Valley, the prime attraction of the east end of Molokai. Here, scented pine forests and groves of fern are set with fruit trees and flowers, and two great waterfalls, including the 250-foot-high Moaula Falls (facing page), cascade into the Halawa Stream (above), which then wanders on to meet the sea at the gently-curving shoreline of Halawa Bay (top).

Since the 1970s, Molokai's western coast has seen the rapid development of tourism, but has nevertheless retained its own special beauty. The Polynesian-style Sheraton Molokai Hotel (facing page bottom), with its low, two-story cottages, stretches itself luxuriously, yet unobtrusively, along Kepuhi Beach (top and facing page top), while the Kaluakoi area still contains miles of unspoilt, golden sand (above and overleaf).

An astounding variety of flowers and blooming shrubs bring splashes of vivid color to the Hawaiian archipelago. Top left: a velvety red hibiscus, the state flower of Hawaii, (top) dainty plumeria alba, (left) a delicate Chilean jasminium, (above) deep pink pentas, and (facing page) the dense flower clusters of the ixora, named for a Malabar Coast deity.

Although it is only the third largest of the Hawaiian Islands, Oahu, which means "The Gathering Place," contains over 75% of Hawaii's people, half of whom live in Honolulu. Becoming a major port for whalers and traders in the 18th century, this prosperous and elegant city was made the state capital in the mid-1800s. In 1969, the state government moved from Iolani Palace to the unusual State Capitol (top left and facing page), the open design of which symbolizes Hawaii's freedom of spirit as well as taking advantage of its fine climate. Overlooking Honolulu's downtown district is the Punchbowl Cemetery (top right), which contains the graves of 24,000 American war dead of World War II, Korea and Vietnam. The state's most famous shrine is the Arizona Memorial (above). This recalls the surprise attack on Pearl Harbor, on December 7, 1941, when several ships were hit and the *U.S.S. Arizona* sunk in a mere five minutes, killing 1,177 men. The rusting wreck can be seen to this day, its hull spanned by the graceful, white bridge of the memorial.

Previous pages: ships off Waikiki Beach (these pages), Ohau's busiest resort area and one of the world's most famous shorelines. Stretching for roughly two miles between the Ala Wai Yacht Harbor and Diamond Head, it is actually a series of distinct beaches, offering the finest swimming in Hawaii and each overlooked by a glamorous jungle of modern hotels.

Previous pages: (left) a vast, lifelike mural makes a surreal scene of the Ala Wai Yacht Harbor, seen from palm-fringed Aina Moana (right), or Magic Island. Facing page: the Waikiki Peninsula and downtown Honolulu, (top) viewed from Diamond Head, which is seen on the horizon (bottom). This page: rosy evening light on a quiet, glamorous Waikiki Beach, which during the day (overleaf) is alive with brightly-colored bathing suits, sails and sunshades.

Facing page bottom: Waikiki and downtown Honolulu seen from the Punchbowl Cemetery. On the horizon looms Oahu's distinctive landmark, Diamond Head, a volcanic crater that has been extinct for around 150,000 years. It was thus named after 19th-century sailors found there some glittering calcite crystals that they believed to be diamonds. Above: palm trees at Waikiki Beach, and (facing page top and overleaf) a forest of masts in Ala Wai Yacht Harbor, seen from the peninsula of Aina Moana.

Since 1937, Waikiki's free Kodak Hula Show has been delighting audiences with all the color and spectacle of traditional Hawaiian entertainment. Dancers (above and facing page bottom), in national dress, sway to the music of ukuleles and guitars, which is provided by *tutus*, or grandmothers (facing page top and overleaf), sporting brightly-patterned gowns called *muumuus*.

Koko Head Regional Park, at the eastern end of Oahu, offers a great variety of coastal scenery, from rugged lava rock formations to gentle, golden stretches of sand. It contains two parks, Sandy Beach Park (this page), which is particularly popular with surfers, and Hanauma Bay Beach Park (facing page), which boasts sparkling blue waters and swaying palm trees. From a lookout point on Diamond Head Road, there is a fine view of Hanauma Bay (overleaf) with Koko Head beyond.

The sensuous folds and valleys (above) of the Koolau Mountains, Oahu's 37-mile-long eastern backbone, create spectacular landscapes where they meet the island's windward coast. Particularly fine are the scenic views from the Pali Lookout (facing page). Overleaf: this rain-soaked area , around Kaneohe Bay (left bottom), is characterized by luxuriant, varied vegetation, especially in the dense rainforest of Nuuanu Valley (left top) and in the green Ahuimanu Valley, the site of the exquisite Byodo-In Temple (right top). This replica of a 900-year-old temple near Kyoto, Japan, stands in beautiful landscaped gardens with a two-acre reflecting pool containing over 10,000 sacred carp (right bottom).

At the small, rural town of Laie, on Oahu's windward coast, are to be found two of Hawaii's most interesting attractions. The elegant Mormon Temple (above and right) was built in 1919 by the Church of Jesus Christ of the LatterDay Saints, a body that is also responsible for the splendid Polynesian Cultural Center. Here, seven different cultures of the South Seas are represented by authentically-recreated villages and spectacular live shows. Facing page center left: the Hawaiian village, and (remaining pictures) the exhilarating "Pageant of the Long Canoes," a show combining all the richness and color of Polynesian traditions, including the Hawaiian *hula* dance, Fijian spear-brandishing and Maori legend.

Above: Waimea Falls, in the lush setting of Waimea Falls Park, near Oahu's northwestern coast. Covering 1,800 acres, the park boasts an arboretum in which flourish a staggering variety of tropical trees, vines, shrubs and flowers, including giant lilypads (facing page). A few miles south of the park is beautiful Waialua Bay (overleaf) near Haleiwa.

Named the "Garden Island" and used as the setting for the film *South Pacific*, Kauai is, to many, the closest thing to paradise on earth. Its varied scenery ranges from the south coast's rocky Makehuena Point (above), near Poipu, to the intriguing Menehune Gardens (top), at Nawiliwili Bay, which contain an array of extraordinary plants, including a giant weeping banyan tree. Lihue, Kauai's financial and cultural center, is one of Hawaii's oldest sugar plantation towns and still ranks among its biggest sugar producers. Facing page: (bottom) the McBryde Sugar Company Cane Fields, and (top) Lihue's finest historic church, the Lutheran Church of the Nations, which was built in 1883 and comprises an interesting mix of New England and Bavarian architecture.

Mark Twain is quoted as having called the Waimea Canyon (previous pages, facing page top and above) the "Grand Canyon of the Pacific." Being 2,875 feet deep, one mile wide and ten miles long, it may not match the size of the Arizona gorge, yet its colors are equally spectacular and, with the ever-shifting cloud patterns and changing light of day, the canyon can appear in soft, pastel blues and greens or deep indigos and emeralds, splashed by the brilliant red of volcanic rock. Another of western Kauai's breathtaking views is that from the 4000-foot-high Kalalau Lookout (facing page bottom), below which the great Kalalau Valley stretches out to the sparkling Na Pali Coast. The main town of this area is historic Waimea (top), Captain Cook's first Hawaiian landing place and a major trading and missionary settlement in the 1800s.

Previous pages: a magnificent view of the Kalalau Valley and Na Pali Coast from Puu O Kila Lookout. Further east along the north coast of Kauai are idyllic beaches typical of the luxuriant beauty of the South Seas. Top: Haena Beach, the graceful, palm-studded curve of golden sand backed by green mountains that was chosen as the *Bali Hai* set for the film *South Pacific*, and (above and facing page bottom) Kee Beach, which is overlooked by the triangular Makana or Fireworks Cliff. Facing page top: the view south from Kealia on the east coast, north of Kapaa. Just inland from Princeville on the north coast is the lovely Hanalei Valley (overleaf), where the tranquil Hanalei River wanders through a rich patchwork of taro fields and grazing land. Bounded by the peaks and folds of dark green mountains, it is a true picture of rural Hawaii.

Midway along the east coast of Kauai is Wailua, an area rich in scenic beauty that was once the revered home of the *alii*, or Hawaiian royalty. Among the treasures of Wailua River State Park are the silvery threads of Opaekaa Falls (previous pages) and Wailua Falls (above), which cascade, sometimes in two falls, over an 80-foot cliff into a deep, round pool. It is said that the ancient chiefs used to dive from this cliff to display their courage. The banks of the Wailua River (facing page top) were once lined with temples where these chiefs performed important ceremonies, and in the bluffs towering above the once sacred waters are the still inviolate graves of the *alii*. Top: the lighthouse on Kilauea Point, and (facing page bottom) the cliffs overlooking Kee Beach, both on the north coast. Overleaf and final page: Fern Grotto, in Wailua River State Park, a great, cool cave framed by pale green fishtail ferns and surrounded by tropical trees and flowers.